Bongos

Victoria Blakemore

For Debra, thank you for all of your guidance and support!

Copyright info/picture credits

Table of Contents

What Are Bongos?

Bongos are large mammals.

They are members of the

same family as antelopes,

sheep, and buffalo.

There are two kinds of bongos:

the eastern lowland bongo

and the western mountain

bongo. They differ in color and

where they live.

Bongos are a reddish brown
color. They have thin, white
stripes along their back.

Size

Bongos are some of the largest African antelopes. They are usually between five and nine feet long. They stand around four feet tall at the shoulder.

Adult bongos often weigh between 300 and 900 pounds.

Bongos have white stripes along their body. The stripes help to break up the color of their coat. This makes them harder to see among the trees.

Male bongos often have a coat that is darker in color. It may be nearly dark brown in color.

Both male and female bongos have horns. Their horns are made from **keratin**, which is what human hair and fingernails are made of.

7

Habitat

Bongos are found in forests.

Some are found in lowland

forests while others are found

in more mountainous forests.

Areas with lots of plants help

them stay safe from predators.

Forests provide them with

places to hide and plenty of

plants to eat.

Range

Bongos are only found on the
continent of Africa.

They are found in countries like Zaire, Sudan, Kenya, Niger, and Liberia.

II

Diet

Like other African antelopes, bongos are **herbivores**. They only eat plants.

Their diet is made up of herbs, grasses, leaves, roots, and bark. They may also eat some fruit.

Bongos spend much of their time **grazing**. They prefer younger and fresher plants.

Bongos have a **prehensile** tongue. It is able to wrap around leaves, branches, and roots. It allows bongos to grasp plants.

They also have a special stomach. It has four **chambers**. Food passes through them and breaks down slowly. This allows bongos to get all of the **nutrients** from their food.

Bongos may **wade** into streams

or rivers to get a drink of water.

It also helps them to cool down.

Communication

Bongos use mainly sound and movement to communicate with each other. Unlike many other animals, they rarely use scent.

They can identify each other by the patterns of their stripes and the size and shape of their horns.

Bongos make sounds like snorts, grunts, and moos. They use a loud bleat as a warning when danger is near.

Movement

Bongos have been **observed** running at speeds of over forty miles per hour. This can be helpful when running from predators.

When moving through the forest, bongos tip their horns back so they don't get caught on plants.

Bongos usually move slowly because they spend a lot of time **grazing**.

Bongo Calves

Bongos usually have one baby. It is called a calf. Mothers leave the herd to have their calf.

Calves stay hidden in the tall grasses for the first week of their lives. Then, they are ready to join the other bongos in the herd.

Calves grow very quickly. Their horns start to grow after a few months.

Bongo Life

Bongos are often seen in groups called herds. A herd may have between five and fifty bongos.

Bongos are very **skittish**. They are very likely to run if something they see or hear scares them.

They are most active at dawn
and dusk. It is easier for them to
hide from predators then.

Predators

Bongos are prey for several large predators like leopards and lions. Pythons and hyenas also hunt bongos.

Bongos can be easy prey because of their bright colors. They spend much of their time in the thick forest where they are harder to find.

Young bongos are more likely

to be caught by predators

than adult bongos.

Population

Lowland bongos may become **endangered** if their population continues to **decline**. There are thought to be about 28,000 left in the wild.

Mountain bongos are **critically endangered**. They may soon be **extinct.**

There are thought to be less

then 150 mountain bongos left

in the wild.

Bongos in Danger

Bongos are facing several threats. One of the biggest is habitat loss. Their habitats are being cut down for farming and building.

Bongos are also hunted and trapped for their meat, horns, and fur.

Hunting bongos is illegal in some places. **Poachers** hunt bongos even though it is illegal.

Helping Bongos

Many groups are working to help bongos. Some focus on education. They hope that people will want to help bongos if they know more about them.

Some bongo habitats have been made into protected areas. They provide bongos with a safe place to live.

Some zoos are raising young bongos and teaching them to survive in the wild. When they are old enough, they are released into the wild to join other bongos.

The goal of these programs is to make sure that they do not become extinct.

Glossary

Chamber: a compartment

Critically Endangered: very close to becoming extinct

Decline: get smaller

Endangered: at risk of becoming extinct

Extinct: when there are no more of an animal left in the wild

Grazing: to feed on growing grass

Herbivore: an animal that eats only plants

Keratin: a hard protein

Nutrient: something in food that helps people, plants, and animals grow

Observed: seen

Poacher: someone who hunts illegally

Prehensile: able to grasp

Skittish: easily startled

Wade: to walk in water

About the Author

Victoria Blakemore is a first grade

teacher in Southwest Florida with a

passion for reading.

You can visit her at

www.elementaryexplorers.com

Also in This Series

Gray Wolves — Victoria Blakemore
Sloths — Victoria Blakemore
Flamingos — Victoria Blakemore
Camels — Victoria Blakemore
Koalas — Victoria Blakemore
Honey Bees — Victoria Blakemore
Pandas — Victoria Blakemore

Pangolins — Victoria Blakemore
White-Tailed Deer — Victoria Blakemore
Orcas — Victoria Blakemore
Giraffes — Victoria Blakemore
Corn — Victoria Blakemore
Meerkats — Victoria Blakemore
Echidnas — Victoria Blakemore

Walruses — Victoria Blakemore
Raccoons — Victoria Blakemore
Bald Eagles — Victoria Blakemore
Apples — Victoria Blakemore
Arctic Foxes — Victoria Blakemore
Red Pandas — Victoria Blakemore
Cassowaries — Victoria Blakemore

Tigers — Victoria Blakemore
Ladybugs — Victoria Blakemore
Moose — Victoria Blakemore
Beluga Whales — Victoria Blakemore
Leopards — Victoria Blakemore
Elephants — Victoria Blakemore
Jellyfish — Victoria Blakemore

Binturongs — Victoria Blakemore
Lions — Victoria Blakemore
Dolphins — Victoria Blakemore
Reindeer — Victoria Blakemore
Hammerhead Sharks — Victoria Blakemore
Hippos — Victoria Blakemore
Pumpkins — Victoria Blakemore

Peafowl — Victoria Blakemore
Chameleons — Victoria Blakemore
Florida Panthers — Victoria Blakemore
Aye-Ayes — Victoria Blakemore
Black Bears — Victoria Blakemore
Cheetahs — Victoria Blakemore
Manatees — Victoria Blakemore

Gingerbread — Victoria Blakemore
Polar Bears — Victoria Blakemore
Hot Chocolate — Victoria Blakemore
Orangutans — Victoria Blakemore
Coyotes — Victoria Blakemore
Marshmallows — Victoria Blakemore
Strawberries — Victoria Blakemore

Also in This Series

Aardvarks	Mako Sharks	Alligators	Frogs	Hedgehogs	Brown Bears	Bongos
Sea Turtles	Quokkas	Muskrats	Zebras	Red Foxes	Ring-Tailed Lemurs	Platypuses
Anteaters	Kangaroos	Rhinos	Jaguars	Wombats	Capybaras	Gorillas
Cats	Skunks	Butterflies	Dingoes	Snow Leopards	African Wild Dogs	Penguins
Whale Sharks	Wolverines	Warthogs	Caracals	Badgers	Seals	Hummingbirds
Pikas	Humpback Whales	Pumas	Lemonade	Llamas	Tulips	Ostriches
Sunflowers	Fennec Foxes	Sea Lions	Squirrels	Roses	Porcupines	Ice Cream

www.ingramcontent.com/pod-product-compliance
Lightning Source LLC
Chambersburg PA
CBHW051250020426
42333CB00025B/3149